ADELE 25

EASY PIANO

T0088783

ISBN 978-1-4950-5653-6

Hal•Leonard®
CORPORATION

7777 W. BLUEMOUND RD. P.O. BOX 13819 MILWAUKEE, WI 53213

Visit Hal Leonard Online at
www.halleonard.com

HELLO

Words and Music by ADELE ADKINS
and GREG KURSTIN

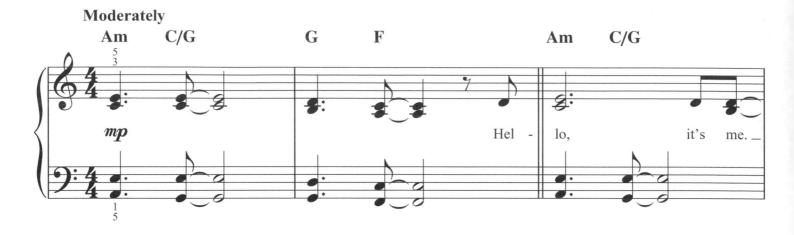

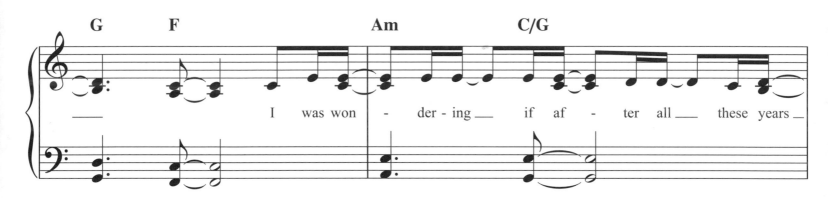

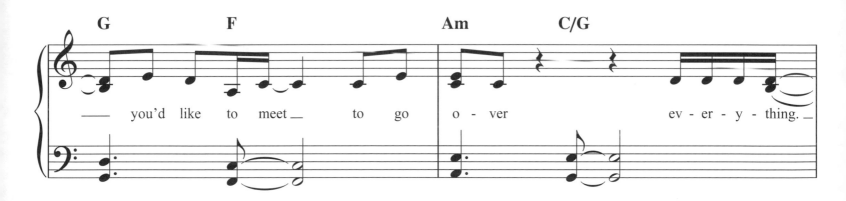

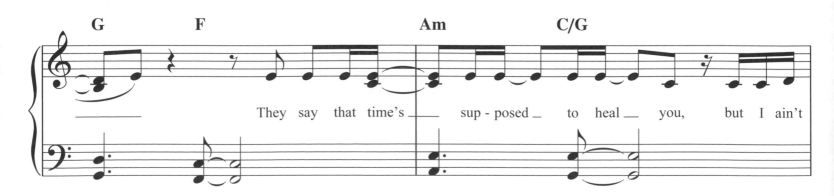

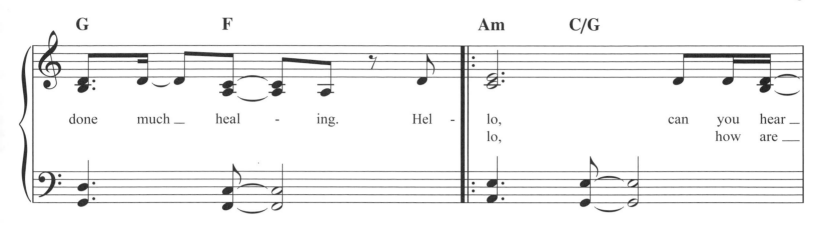

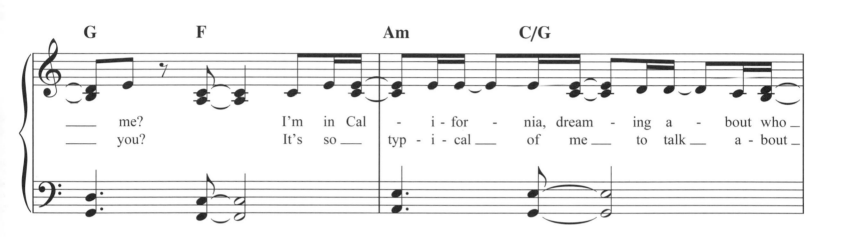

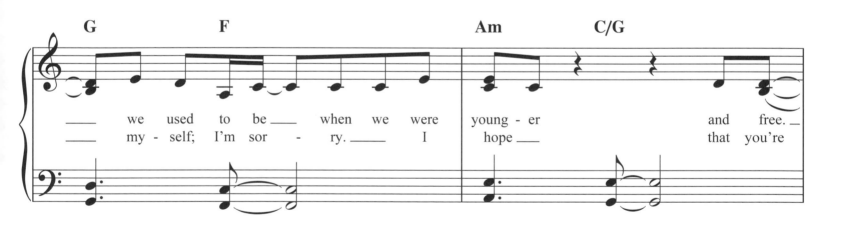

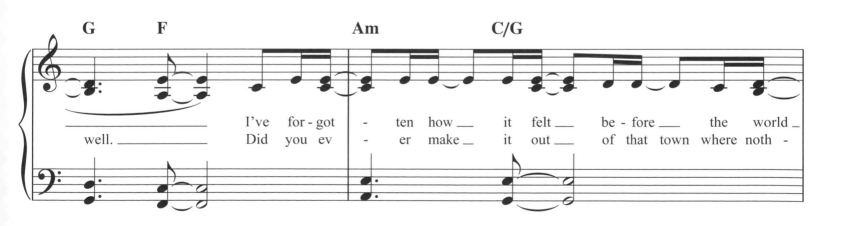

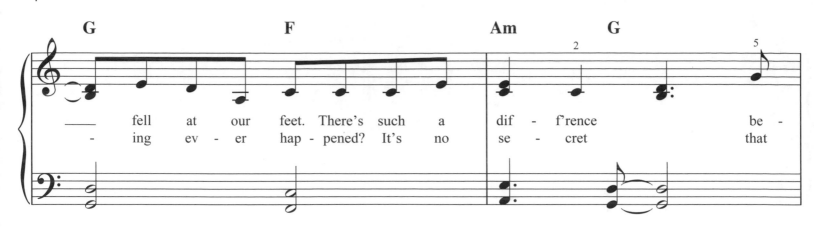

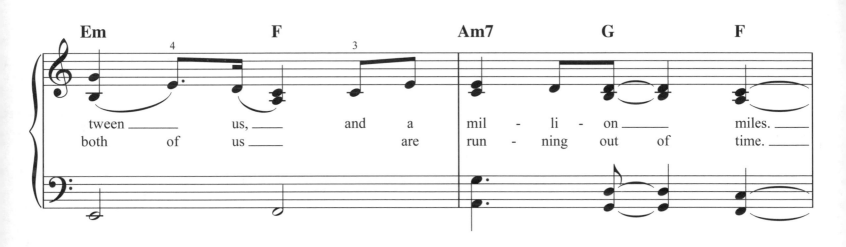

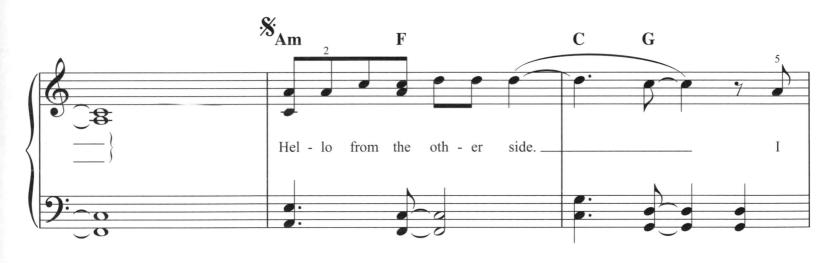

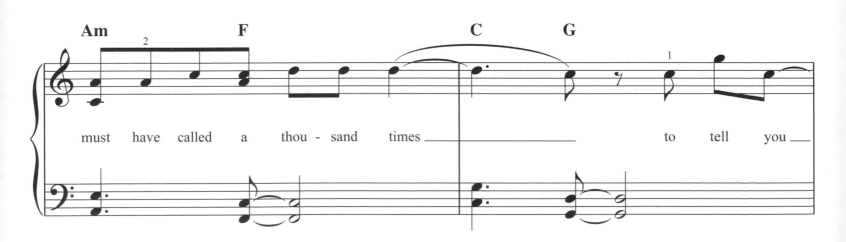

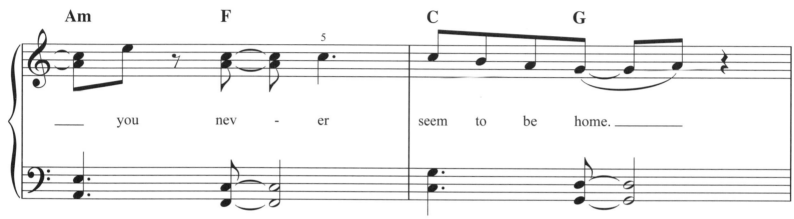

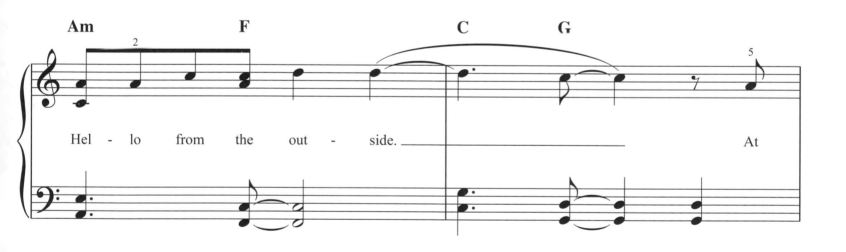

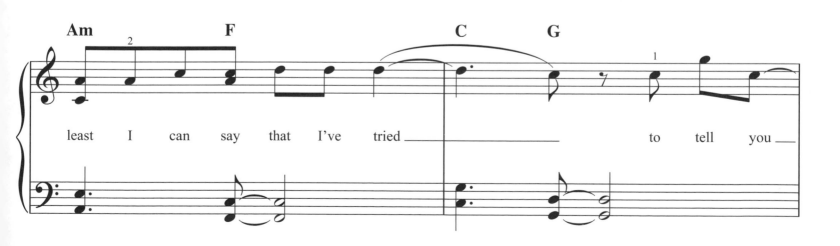

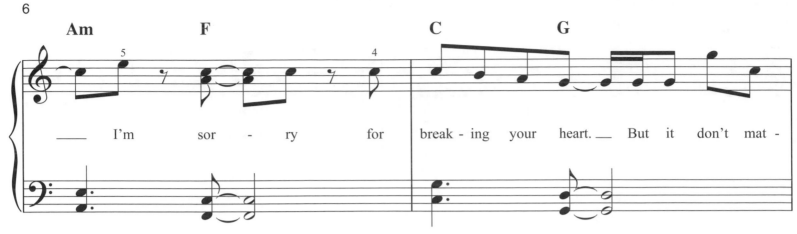

___ I'm sor - ry for break - ing your heart.__ But it don't mat -_

To Coda ⊕

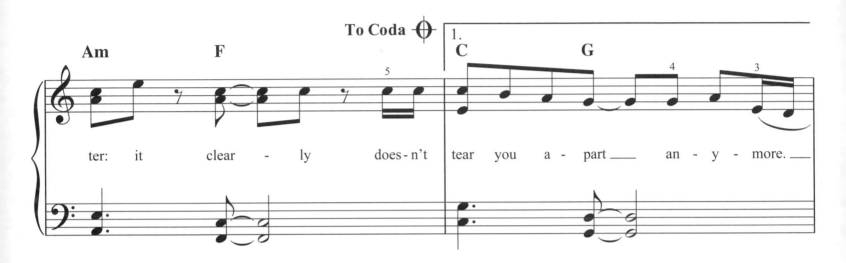

_ter: it clear - ly does - n't tear you a - part__ an - y - more.___

___ Hel -_

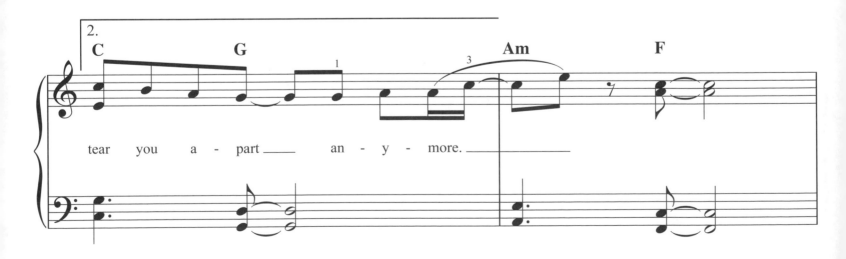

_tear you a - part__ an - y - more.___

7

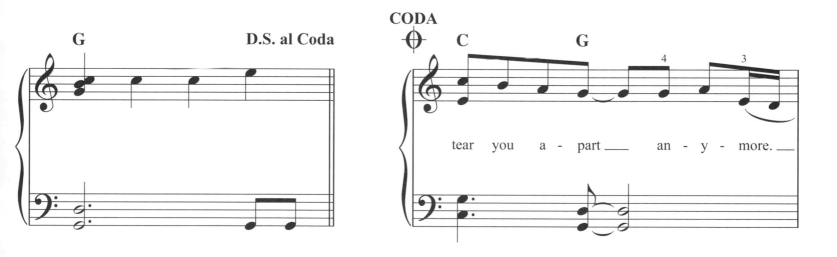

tear you a - part ___ an - y - more. ___

SEND MY LOVE
(TO YOUR NEW LOVER)

Words and Music by ADELE ADKINS,
MAX MARTIN and SHELLBACK

This was all you, none of it me, you put your hands on, _ on my bod - y and
I was too strong, you were trem - bling, you could - n't han - dle _ the hot heat _

told _ me, mm, _ told me you were read - y
ris - ing, mm, _ ba - by, I'm still ris - ing.

for the big one,   for the big jump,   I'd be your last love, _   ev - er - last - ing,
I was run - ning,   you were walk - ing,   you could-n't keep up, __   you were fall - ing

you _____ and me,   mm, _____   that was what you told me.
down, _____   mm, _____   there's on - ly one way down.

I'm   giv - ing you _____ up,   I've   for - giv - en it _____ all, _

_____ you set me _ free. _

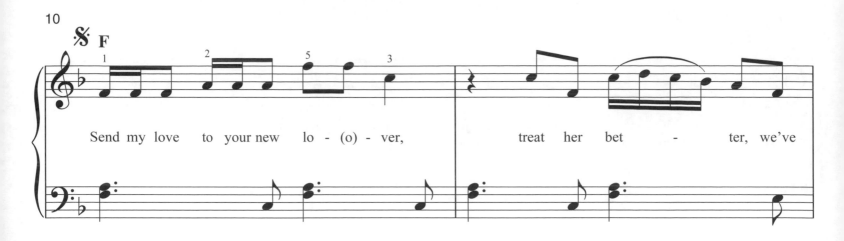

Send my love to your new lo - (o) - ver, treat her bet - ter, we've

got - ta let go of all of our ghosts, ___ we both know we ain't kids no more. ___

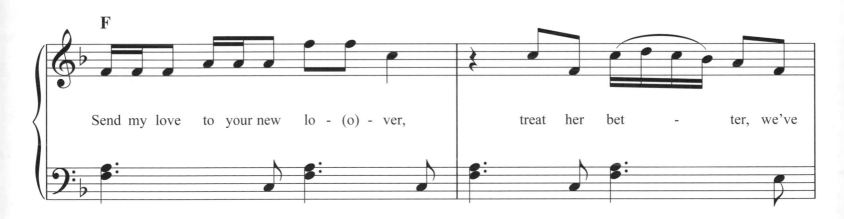

Send my love to your new lo - (o) - ver, treat her bet - ter, we've

To Coda

got - ta let go of all of our ghosts, ___ we both know we ain't kids no more. ___

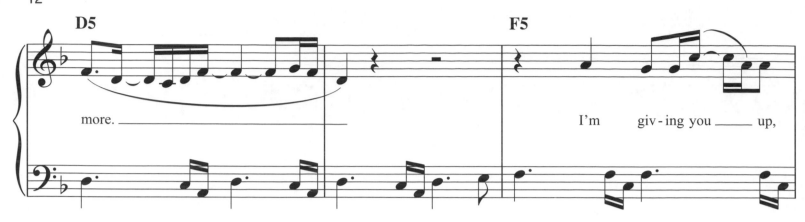

D.S. al Coda

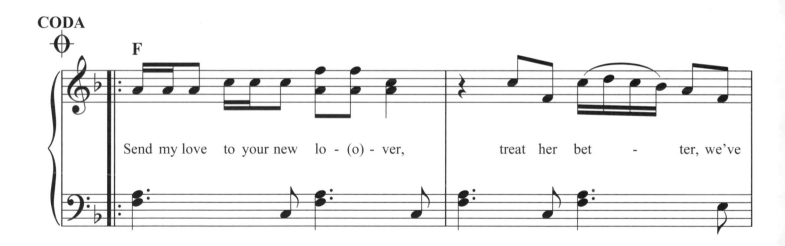

WATER UNDER THE BRIDGE

Words and Music by ADELE ADKINS
and GREGORY KURSTIN

don't pre-tend that you don't want me. Our love ain't wa-ter un-der the

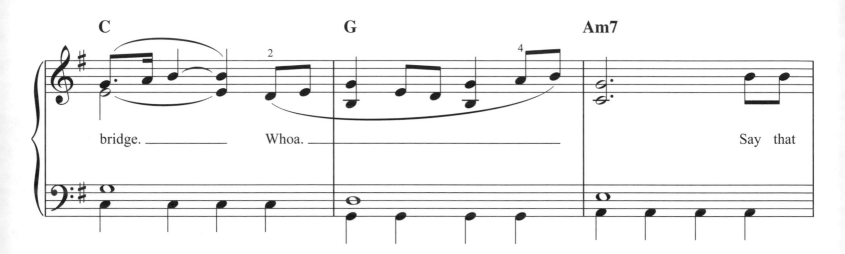

bridge. _____ Whoa. _____ Say that

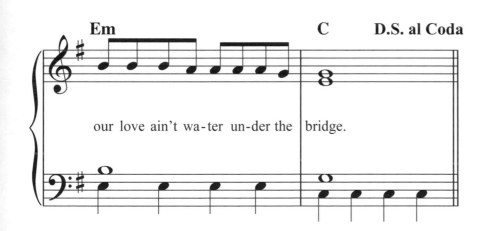

our love ain't wa-ter un-der the bridge.

let me down, let me down gent-ly,

don't pre-tend that you don't want me. Our love ain't wa-ter un-der the

bridge. _____ If you're gon - na let me down, let me down gent - ly,

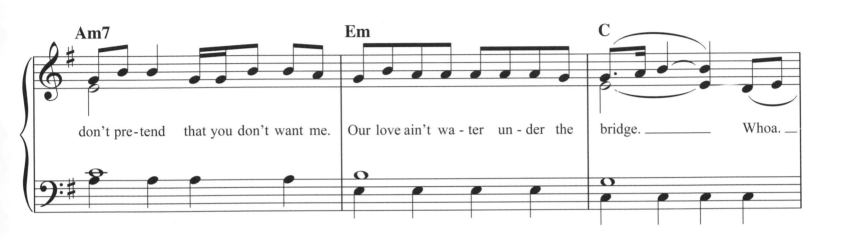

don't pre-tend that you don't want me. Our love ain't wa - ter un - der the bridge. _____ Whoa. _____

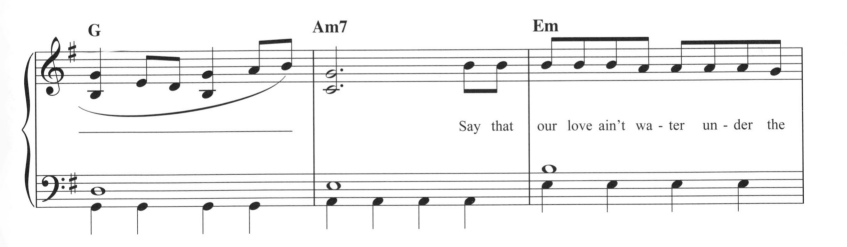

_____ Say that our love ain't wa - ter un - der the

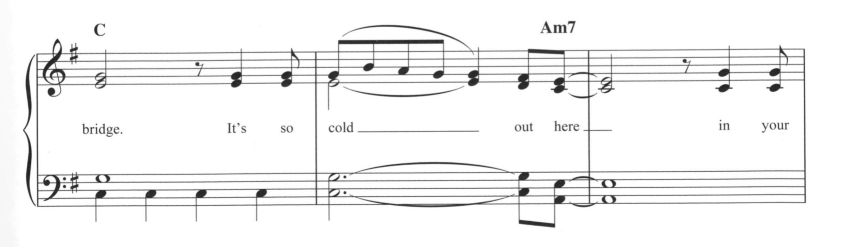

bridge. It's so cold _____ out here _____ in your

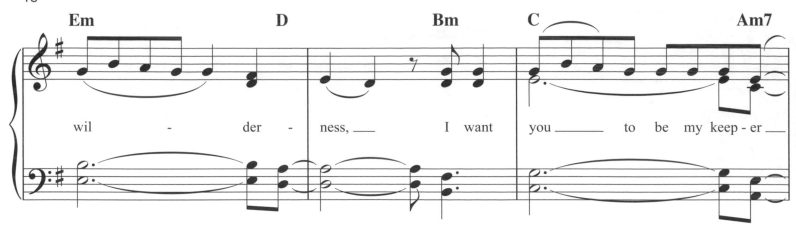

wil - der - ness, ___ I want you ___ to be my keep - er

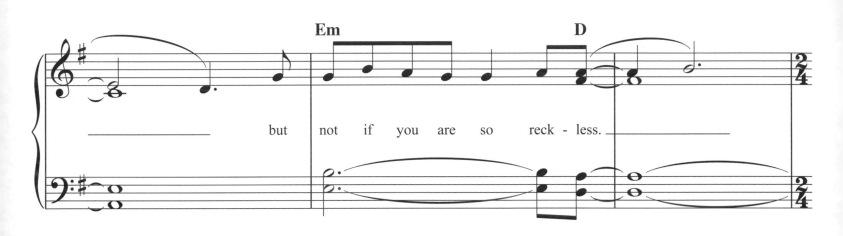

___ but not if you are so reck - less. ___

If you're gon - na let me down, let me down gent - ly, don't pre - tend that you don't want me.

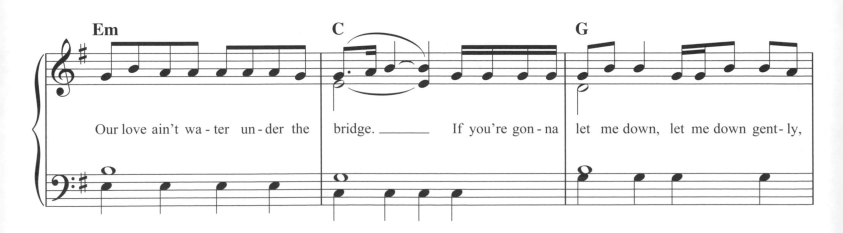

Our love ain't wa - ter un - der the bridge. ___ If you're gon - na let me down, let me down gent - ly,

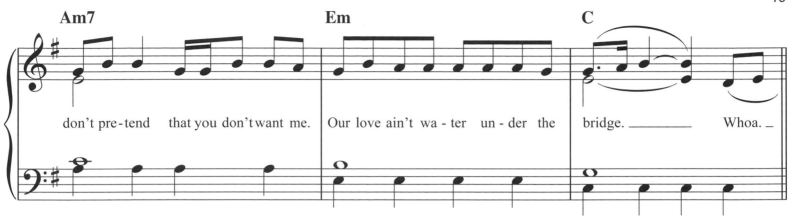

don't pre-tend   that you don't want me.   Our love ain't wa - ter un - der the   bridge. _____   Whoa. _

_____   Say that   our love ain't wa - ter   un - der the

1.   bridge.   Whoa. _____   2.   bridge.

Say that   our love ain't wa - ter   un - der the   bridge.

I MISS YOU

Words and Music by ADELE ADKINS
and PAUL EPWORTH

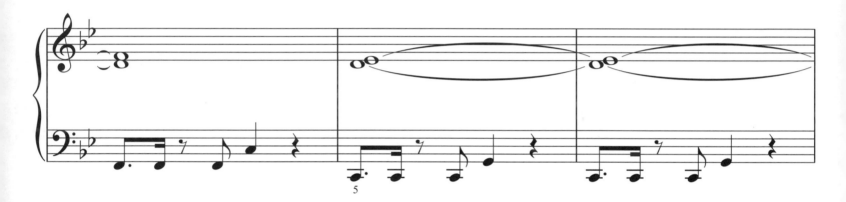

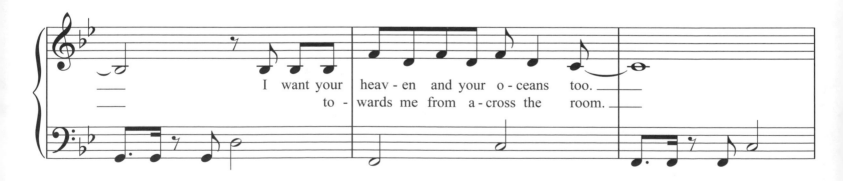

Treat me soft but touch me cruel, I want to teach you things you nev-er knew,
Brush-ing past my ev-'ry groove, no one has me like you do,

ooh ba-by. Bring the floor up to my knees, let me
ooh ba-by. Bring your heart, I'll bring my soul but be

fall in-to your gra-vi-ty. Then kiss me back to life to see
de-li-cate with my e-go. I want to step in-to your great un-known,

your bod-y stand-ing o-ver me. Ba-by, don't let the lights go
with you and me set-ting the tone.

down.

Ba - by, don't let the lights go down.

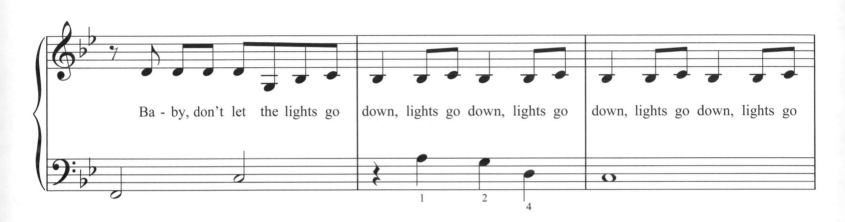

Ba - by, don't let the lights go down, lights go down, lights go down, lights go down, lights go down, lights go

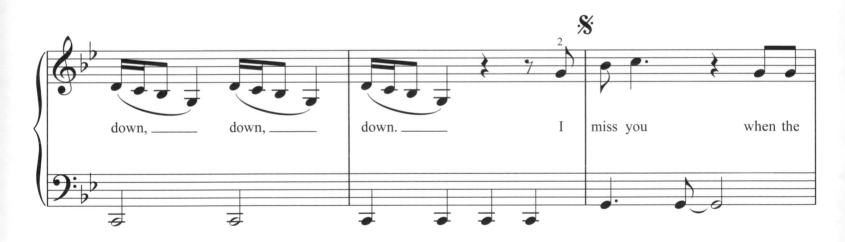

down, _____ down, _____ down. _____ I miss you when the

lights go out, it il - lu - mi - nates all of my doubts. _____

Pull me in, _____ hold me tight, ___ don't let go, _____ ba - by,

give me light. ___ I miss you when the lights go out, it il -

lu - mi - nates all of my doubts. __ Pull me in, _____

To Coda ⊕

hold me tight, ___ don't let go, _____ ba - by, give me light. ___

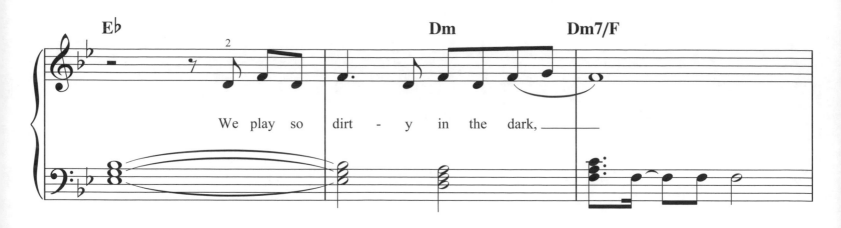

We play so dirt - y in the dark, _____

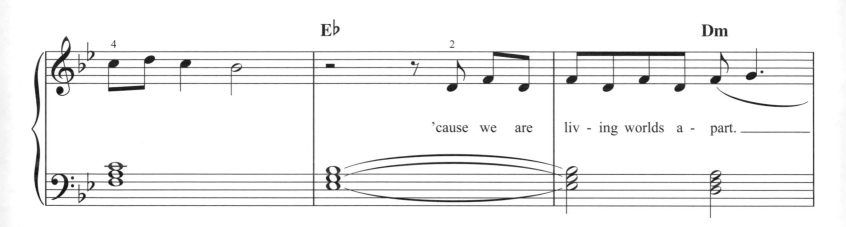

'cause we are liv - ing worlds a - part. _____

_____ It on - ly makes it

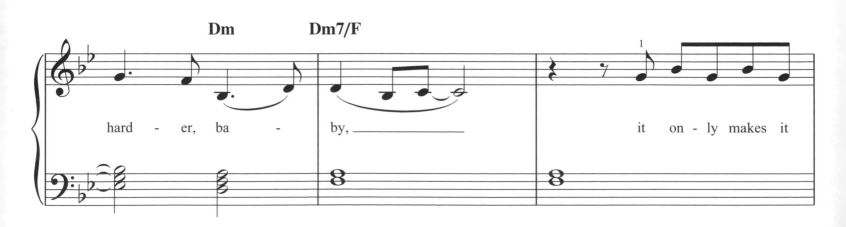

hard - er, ba - by, _____ it on - ly makes it

WHEN WE WERE YOUNG

Words and Music by ADELE ADKINS
and TOBIAS JESSO JR.

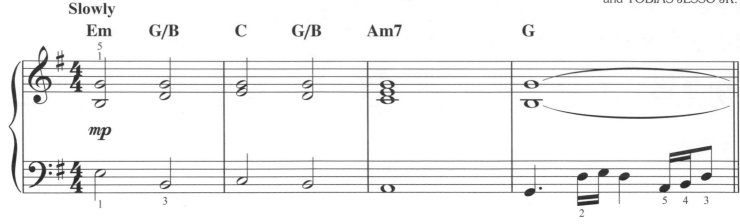

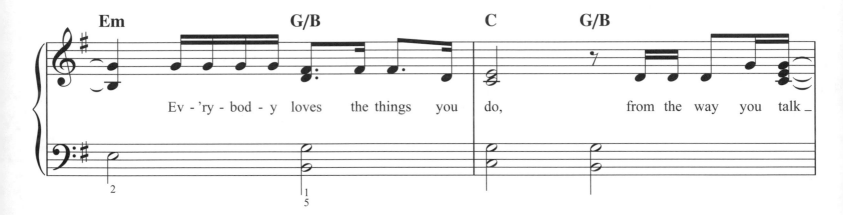

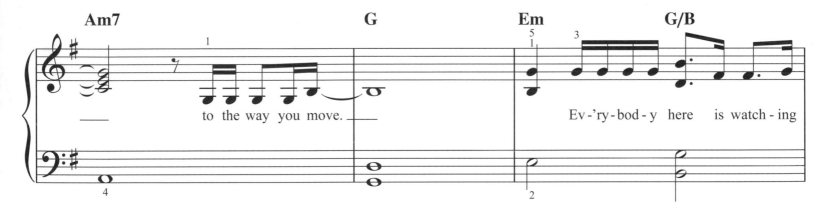

But if by chance you're here a - lone,   can I have a mo - ment   be - fore I
I was so scared to face my fears,   'cause no-bod-y told ____ me   that you'd be

go? _____   'Cause I've been by my - self all night long,   hop - ing you're
here. _____   And I swear you'd moved o - ver - seas: that's what you

some - one ____ I used to know.   You look like a mov - ie,   you sound like a
said _____ when you left me.   You still look like a mov - ie,   you still sound like a

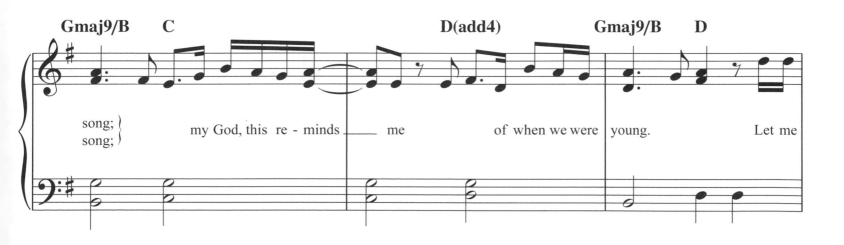

song; }
song; }   my God, this re - minds ____ me   of when we were young.   Let me

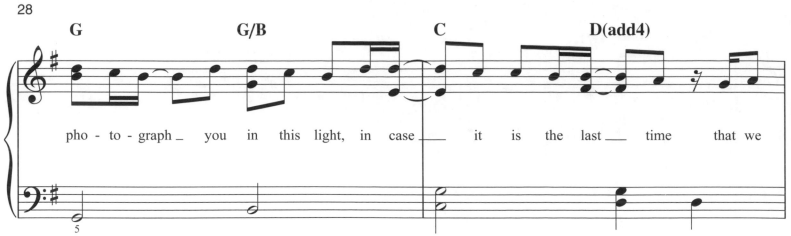

pho - to - graph ___ you in this light, in case ___ it is the last ___ time that we

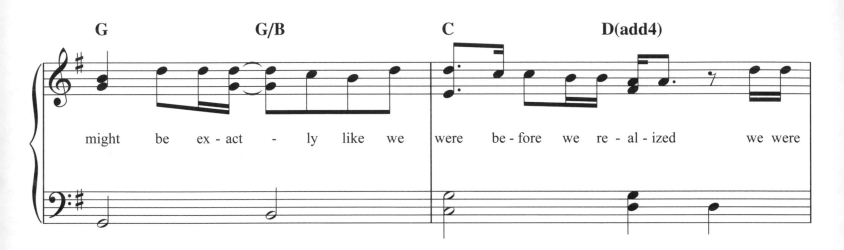

might be ex - act - ly like we were be - fore we re - al - ized ___ we were

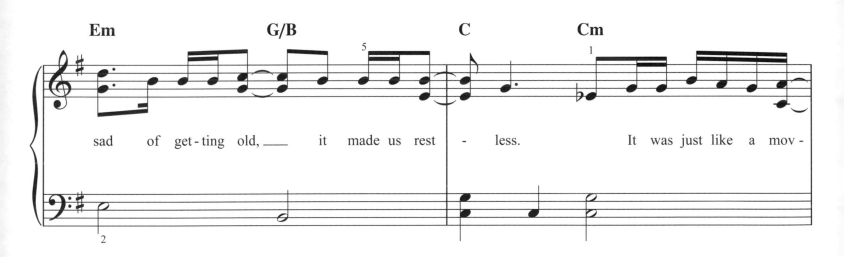

sad of get - ting old, ___ it made us rest - less. It was just like a mov -

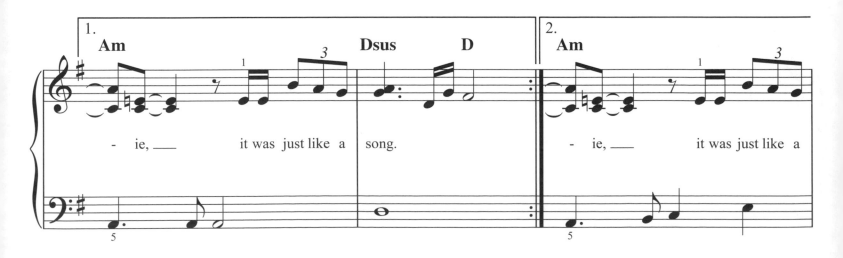

1. - ie, ___ it was just like a song.

2. - ie, ___ it was just like a

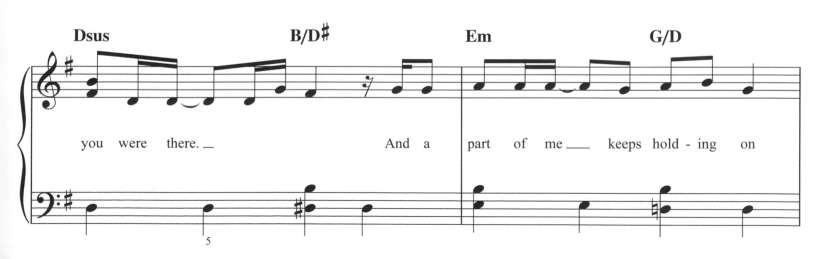

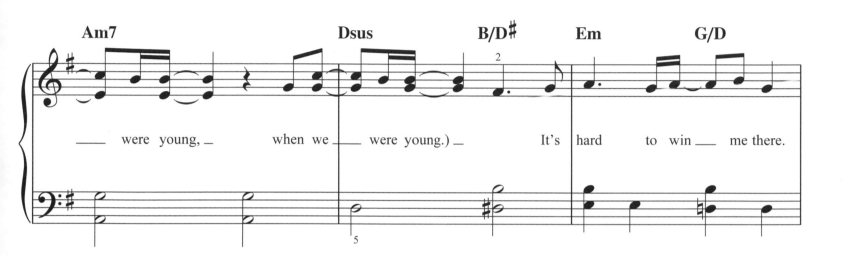

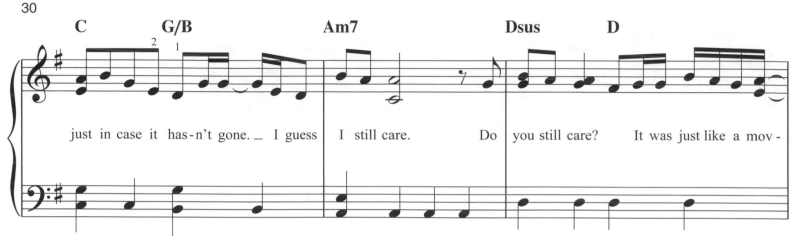

just in case it has-n't gone. _ I guess I still care. Do you still care? It was just like a mov-

- ie, it was just like a song. My God, this re-minds _ me of when we were

young. _____ (When we were young, _ when we _ were young, _ when we _

_ were young, _ when we _ were young.) _ Let me pho-to-graph _ you in this light, in case _

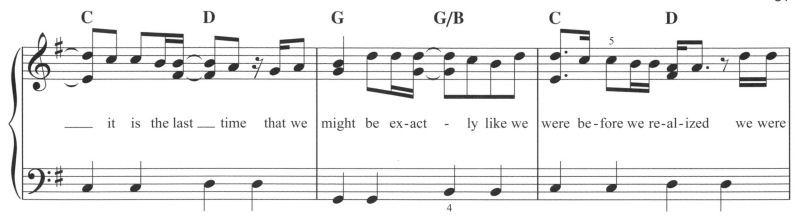

_____ it is the last ___ time that we might be ex-act - ly like we were be-fore we re-al-ized we were

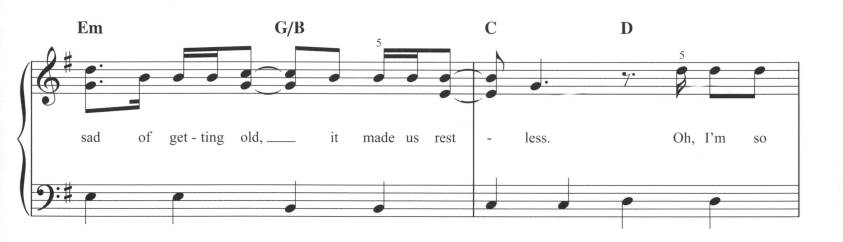

sad of get-ting old, _____ it made us rest - less. Oh, I'm so

mad at get-ting old, _____ it makes me reck - less. It was just like a mov-

- ie, it was just like a song _____ when we were young.

REMEDY

Words and Music by ADELE ADKINS
and RYAN TEDDER

fore my eyes ___ I saw, _____ my heart it came ___ to
love, it is ___ my truth _____ and I will al - ways love

life. ___ This ain't eas - y, it's not meant to ___ be. Ev - 'ry
you, ___ love ___ you. When the

first time only

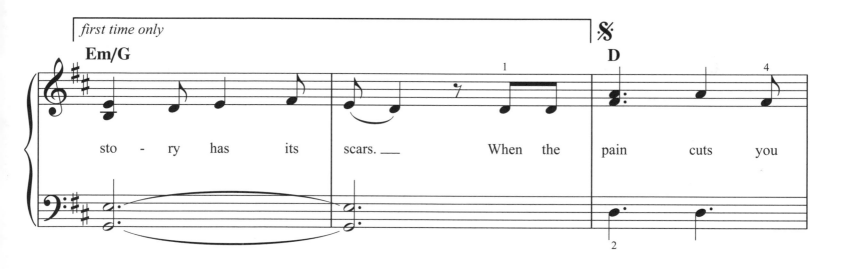

sto - ry has its scars. ___ When the pain cuts you

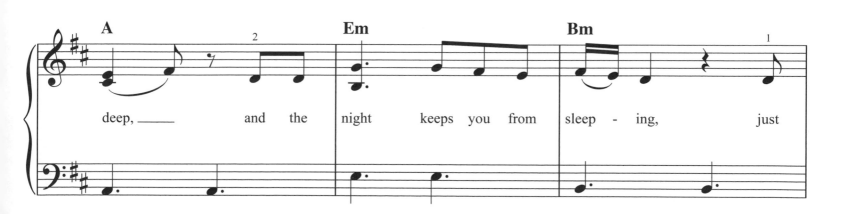

deep, ___ and the night keeps you from sleep - ing, just

look and you will see that I _____ will be your rem - e -

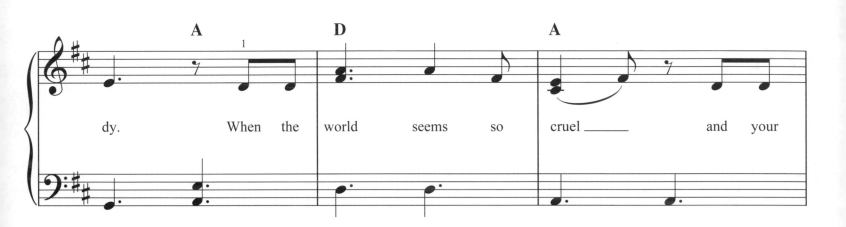

dy. When the world seems so cruel _____ and your

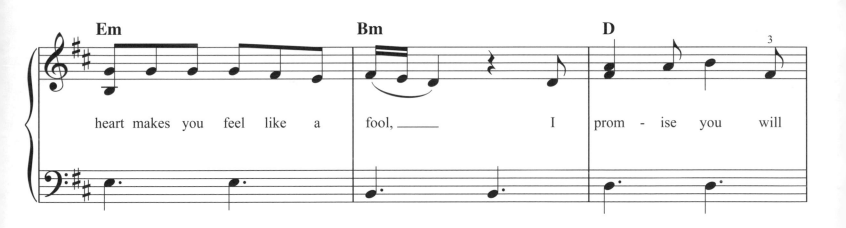

heart makes you feel like a fool, _____ I prom - ise you will

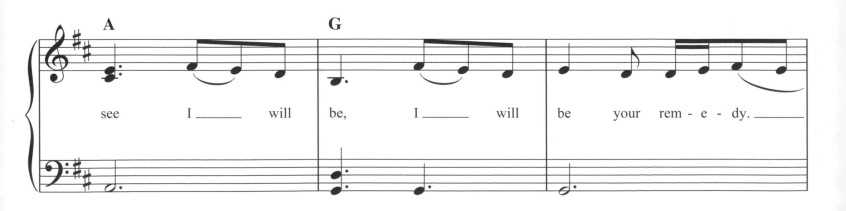

see I _____ will be, I _____ will be your rem - e - dy. _____

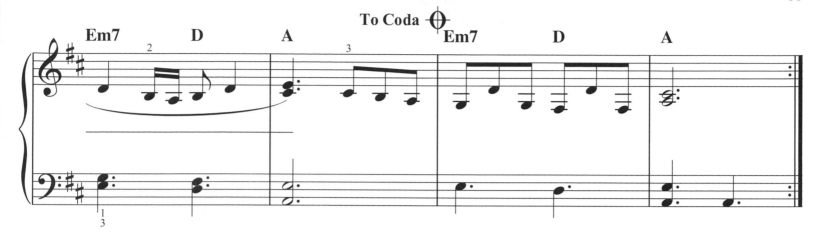

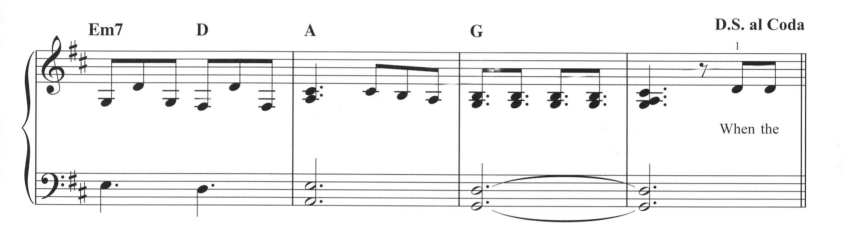

When the

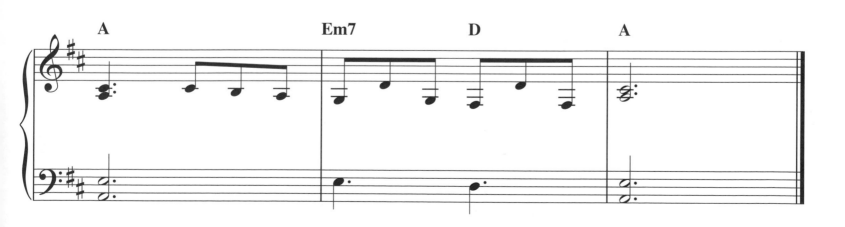

RIVER LEA

Words and Music by ADELE ADKINS
and BRIAN BURTON

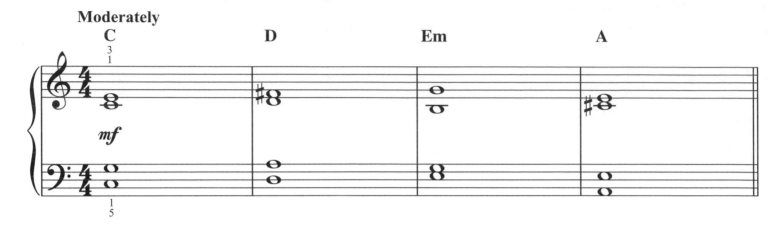

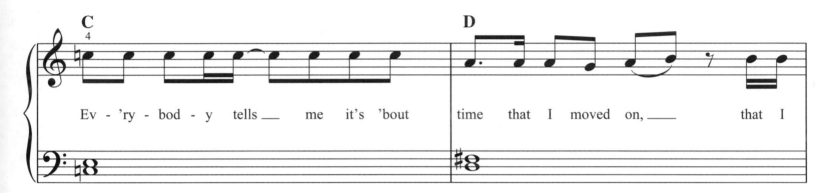

Ev - 'ry - bod - y tells __ me it's 'bout time that I moved on, __ that I

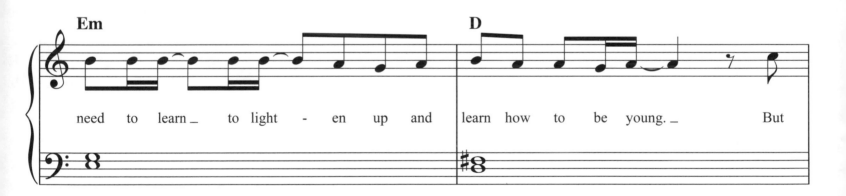

need to learn __ to light - en up and learn how to be young. __ But

my heart is a val - ley, it's so shal - low and man - made, __ I'm

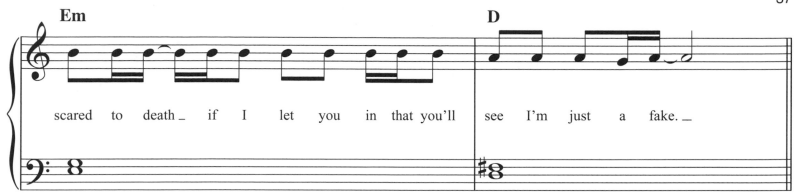

scared to death _ if I let you in that you'll see I'm just a fake. _

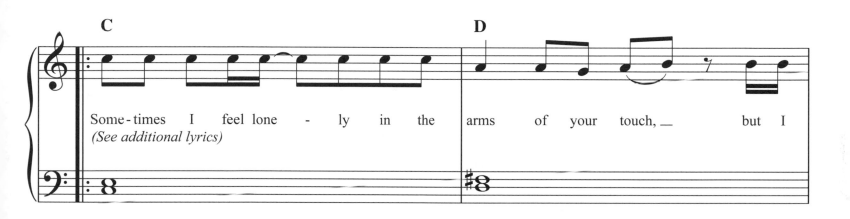

Some-times I feel lone - ly in the arms of your touch, _ but I
(See additional lyrics)

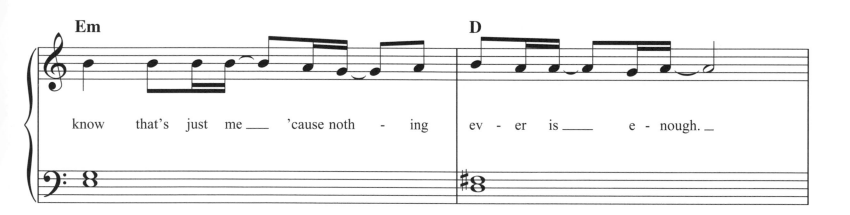

know that's just me _ 'cause noth - ing ev - er is _ e - nough. _

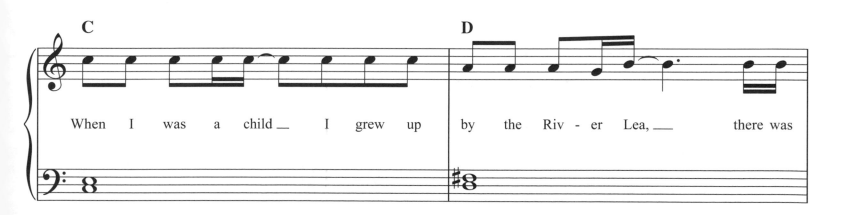

When I was a child _ I grew up by the Riv - er Lea, _ there was

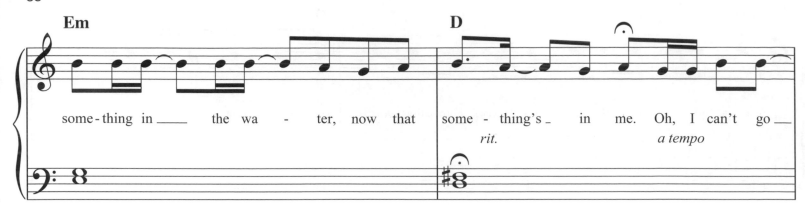

some-thing in _____ the wa - ter, now that some - thing's _ in me. Oh, I can't go _____

rit. *a tempo*

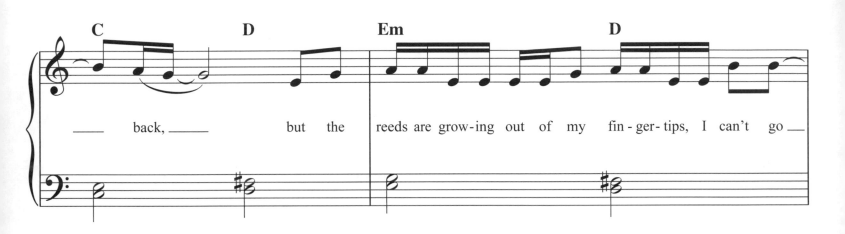

_____ back, _____ but the reeds are grow-ing out of my fin-ger-tips, I can't go _____

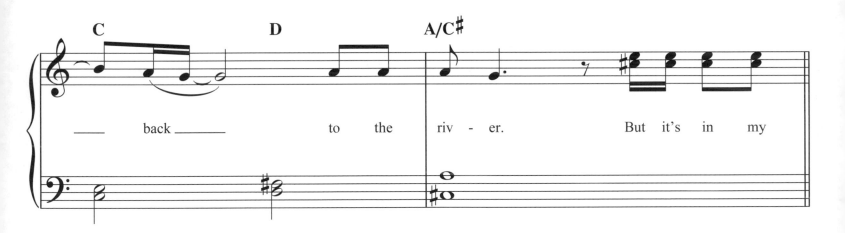

_____ back _____ to the riv - er. But it's in my

roots, in my veins, it's in my blood and I stain ev - 'ry

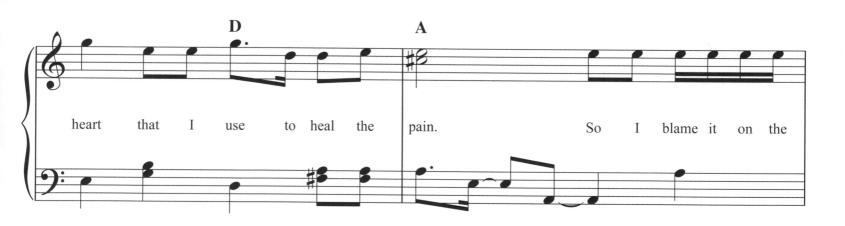

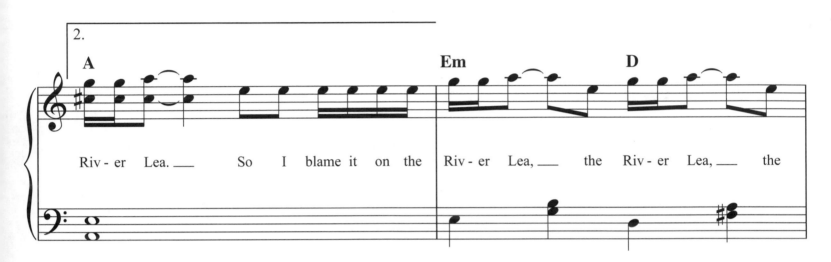

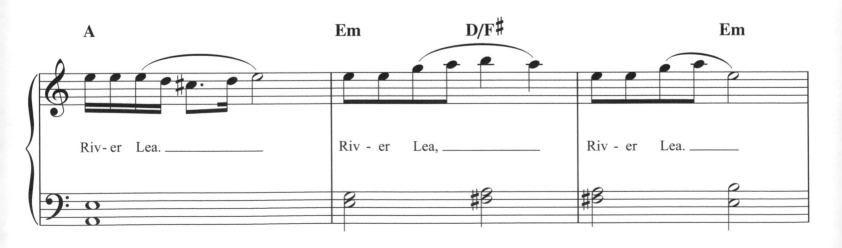

Additional Lyrics

I should prob'ly tell you now before it's way too late,
That I never meant to hurt you or lie straight to your face.
Consider this my apology, I know it's years in advance
But I'd rather say it now in case I never get the chance.

LOVE IN THE DARK

Words and Music by ADELE ADKINS
and SAMUEL DIXON

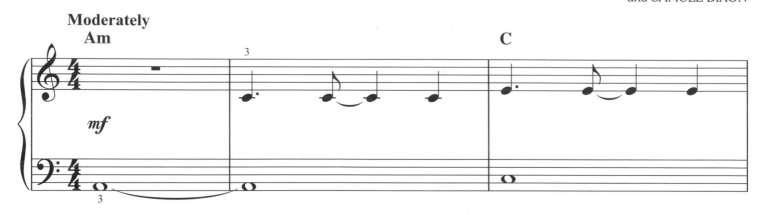

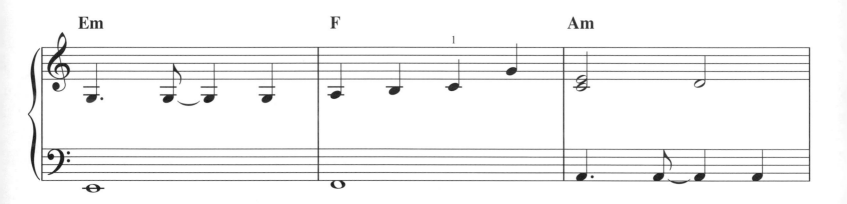

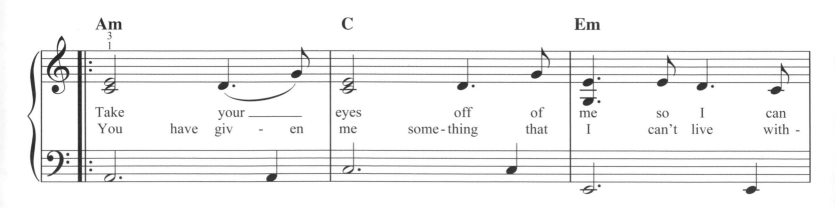

Take your _____ eyes off of me so I can
You have giv - en me some-thing of that I can't live with -

F   Am   C

leave,   I'm   far   too   a -   shamed   to   do   it

out,   you   must -   n't   un -   der -   es -   ti -   mate   that

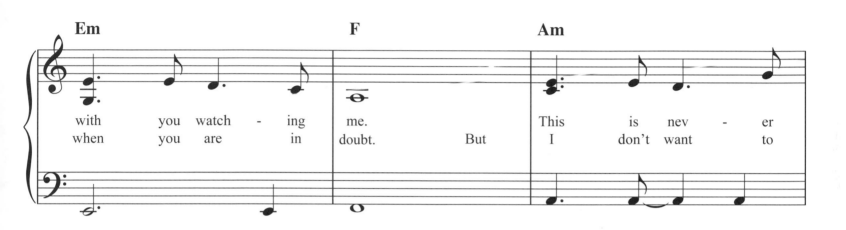

Em   F   Am

with   you   watch -   ing   me.   This   is   nev -   er

when   you   are   in   doubt.   But   I   don't   want   to

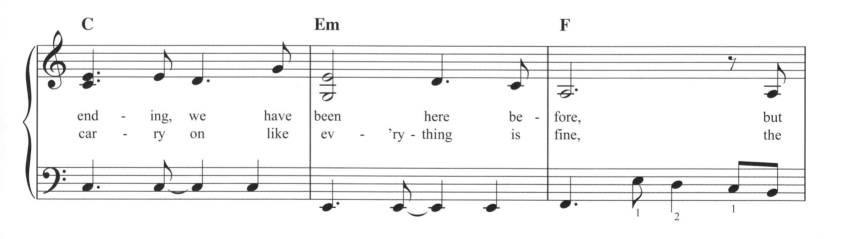

C   Em   F

end -   ing,   we   have   been   here   be -   fore,   but

car -   ry   on   like   ev -   'ry - thing   is   fine,   the

Am   C   Em

I   can't   stay   this   time   'cause   I   don't   love   you   an -   y -

long -   er   we   ig -   nore   it   all   the   more   that   we   will

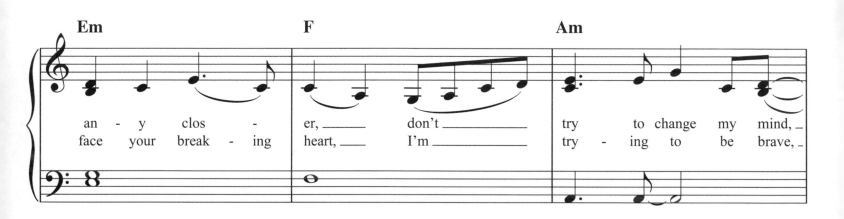

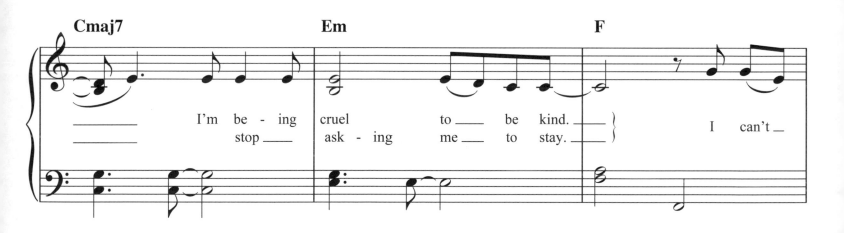

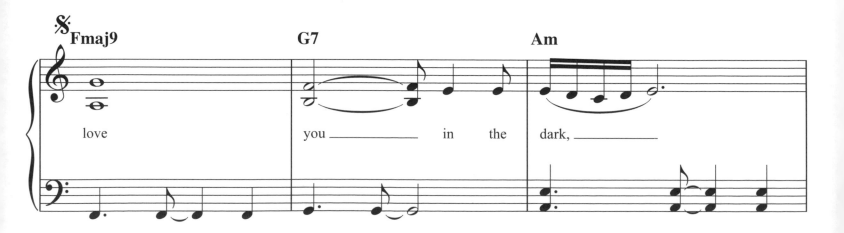

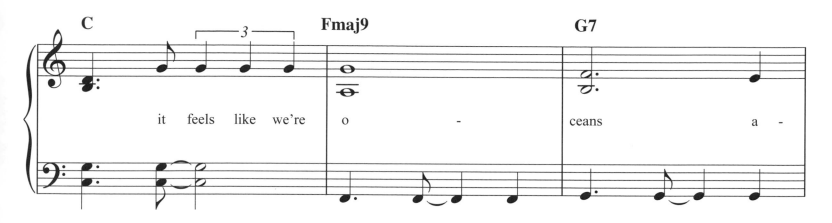

it feels like we're o - ceans a -

part. _____ There is so ___ much space be - tween ___

___ us, ba - by, we're al - read - y de - feat - ed, yeah,

To Coda ⊕

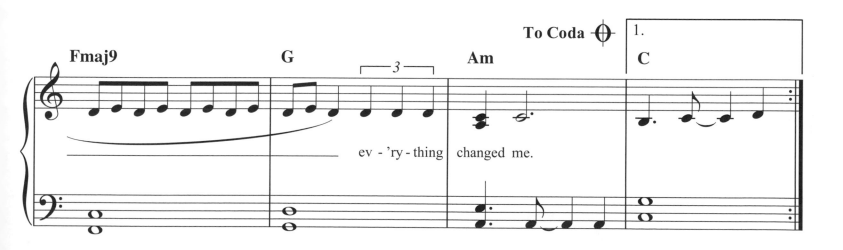

ev - 'ry - thing changed me.

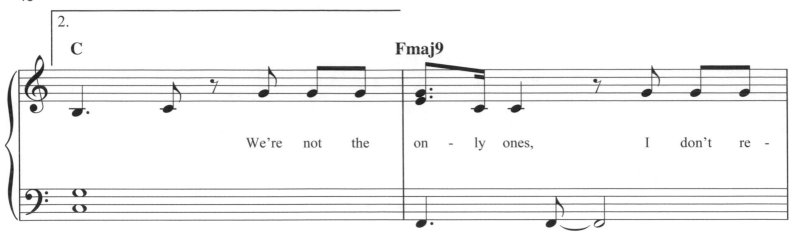

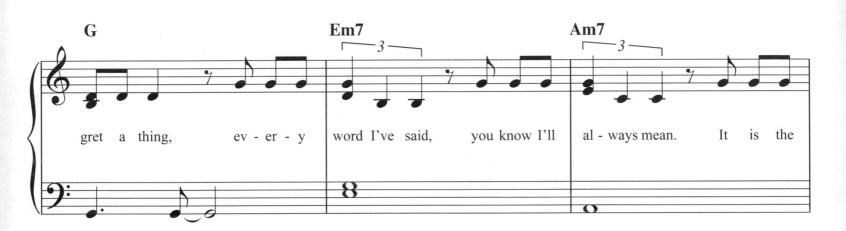

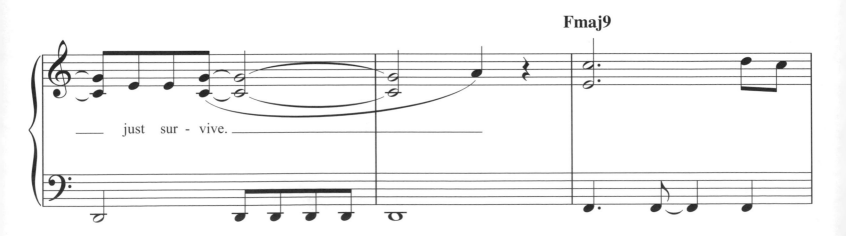

That's why I can't

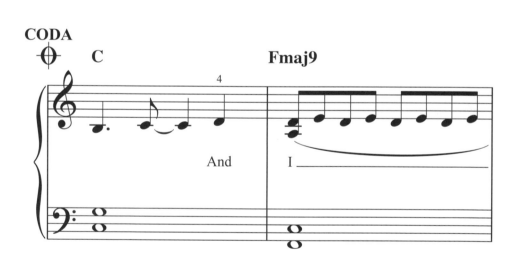

And I _____

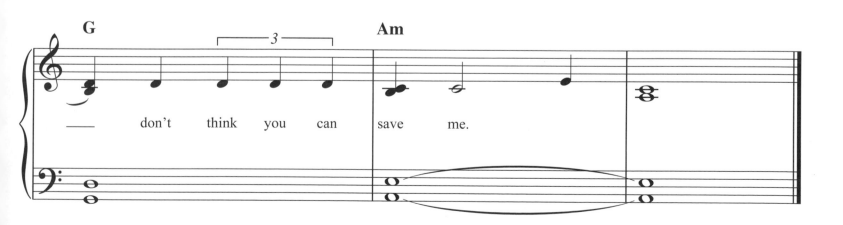

_____ don't think you can save me.

MILLION YEARS AGO

Words and Music by ADELE ADKINS
and GREGORY KURSTIN

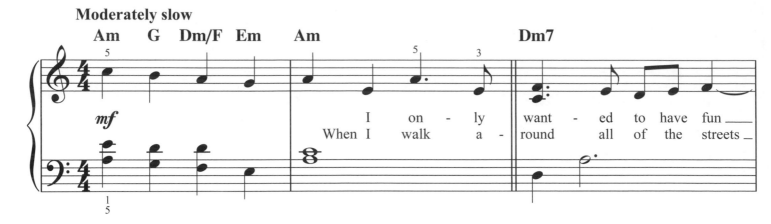

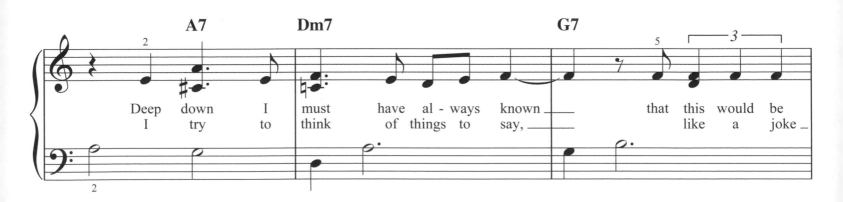

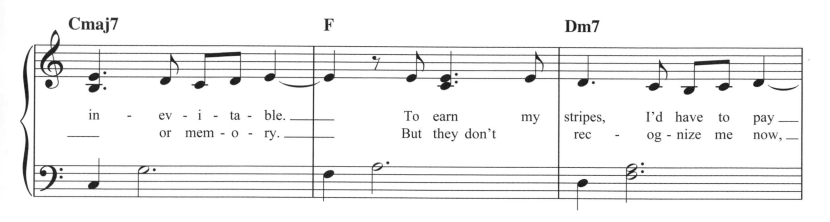

in - ev - i - ta - ble. ___ To earn my stripes, I'd have to pay ___

___ or mem - o - ry. ___ But they don't rec - og - nize me now, ___

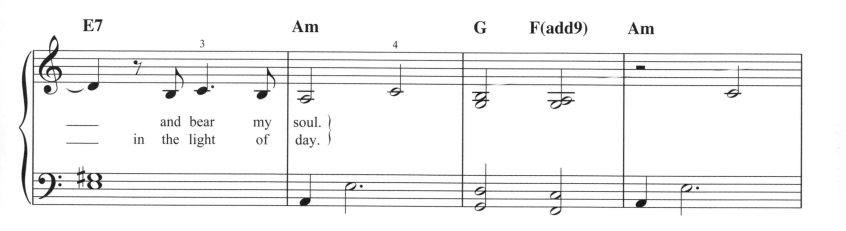

___ and bear my soul.

___ in the light of day.

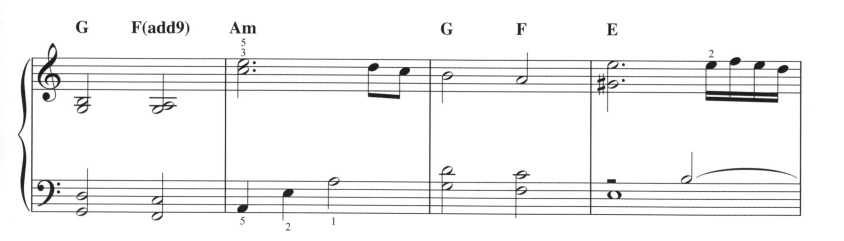

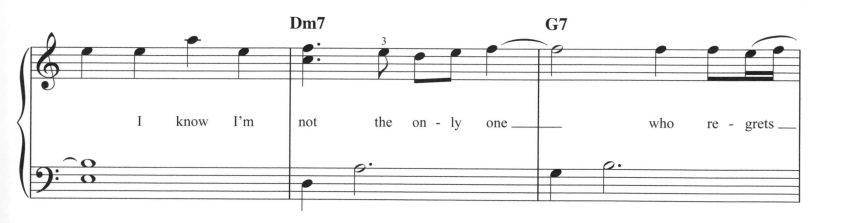

I know I'm not the on - ly one ___ who re - grets ___

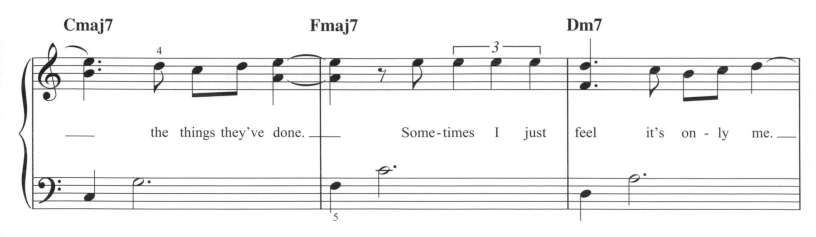

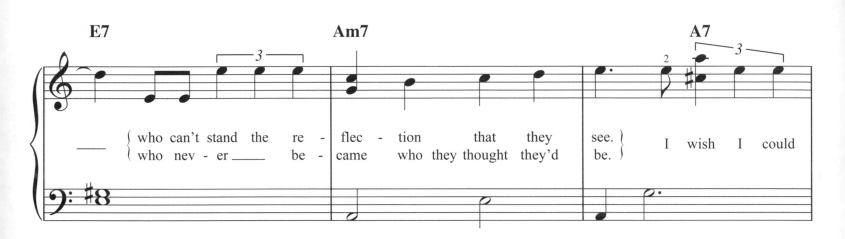

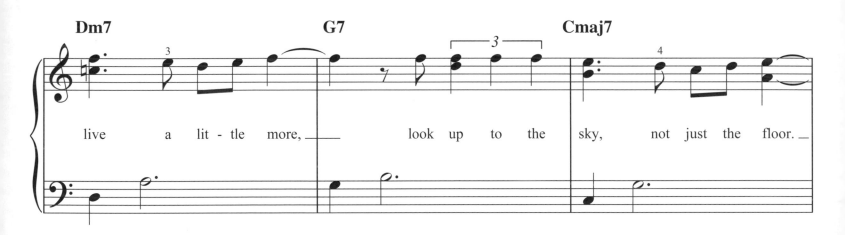

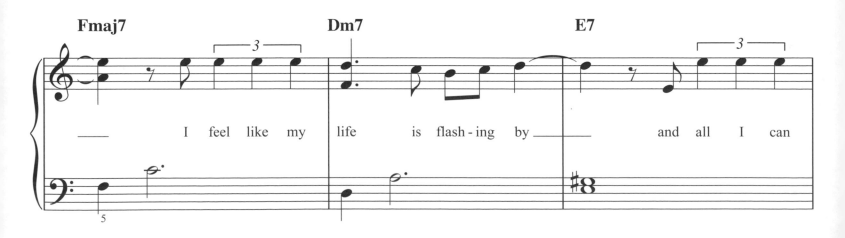

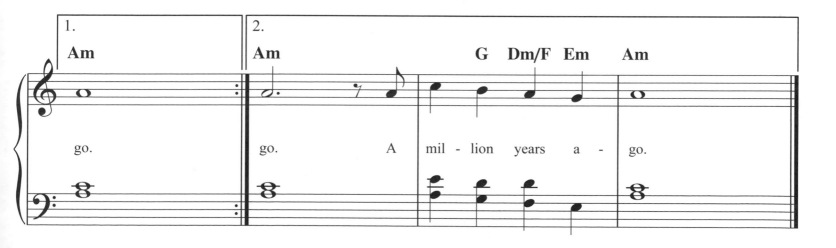

ALL I ASK

Words and Music by ADELE ADKINS,
PHILIP LAWRENCE, BRUNO MARS
and CHRIS BROWN

Moderately fast

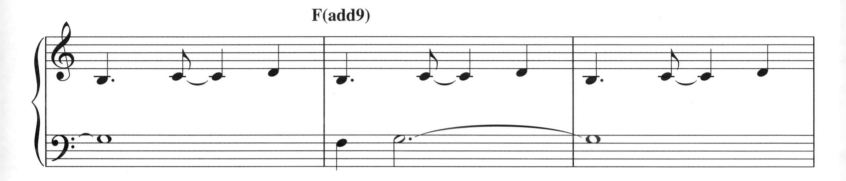

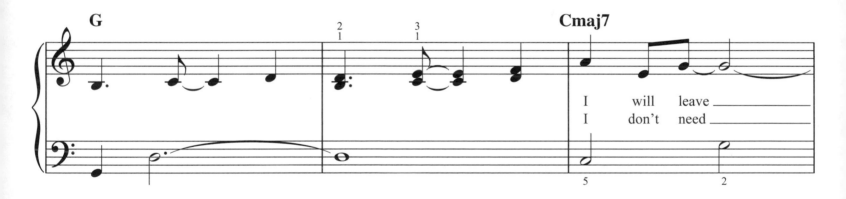

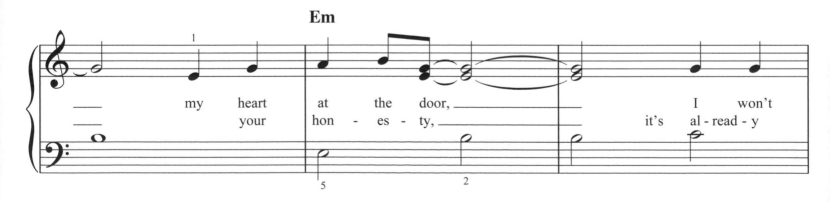

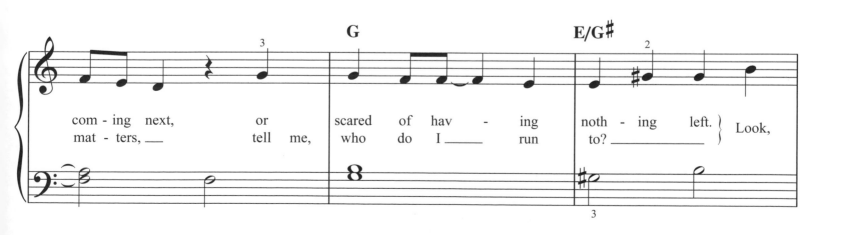

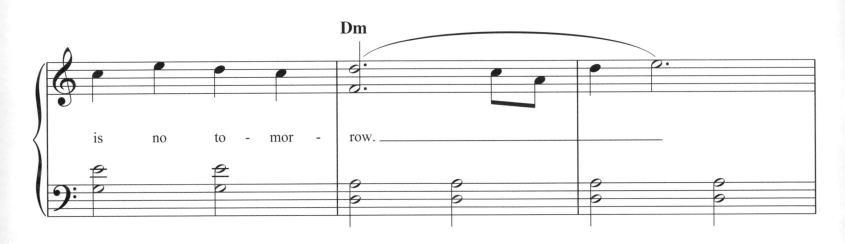

hold me like ___ I'm more than just a friend. ___

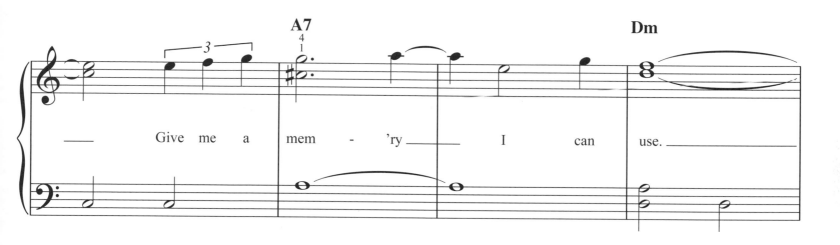

Give me a mem - 'ry ___ I can use. ___

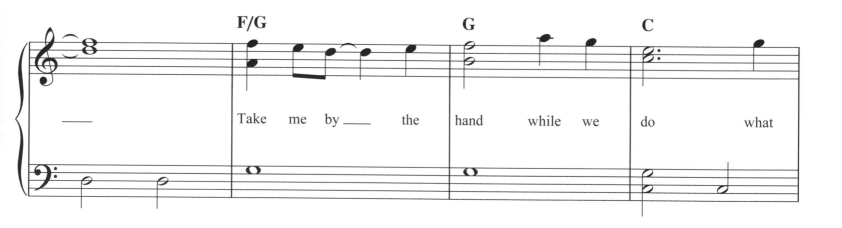

Take me by ___ the hand while we do what

lov - ers ___ do, it mat - ters how ___ this ends. ___

To Coda ⊕ **1.**

F/G   Cmaj7

'Cause what if I nev-er love _____ a - gain? _____

2.

F/G   C/B♭

what if I nev-er love _____ a - gain? _____

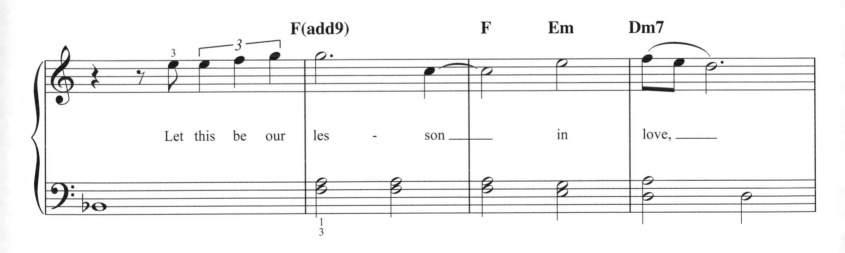

F(add9)   F   Em   Dm7

Let this be our les - son _____ in love, _____

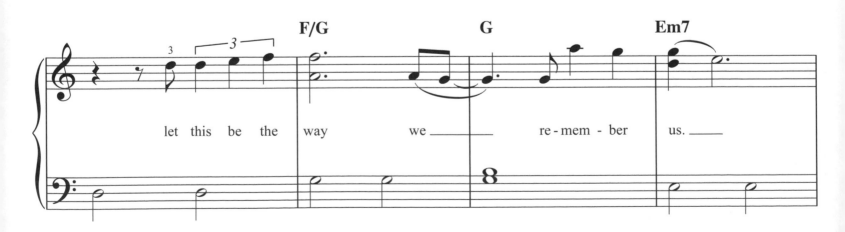

F/G   G   Em7

let this be the way we _____ re-mem-ber us. _____

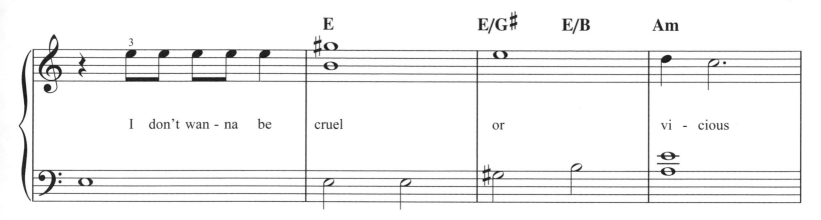

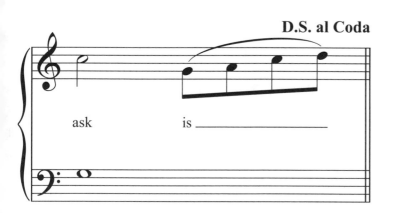

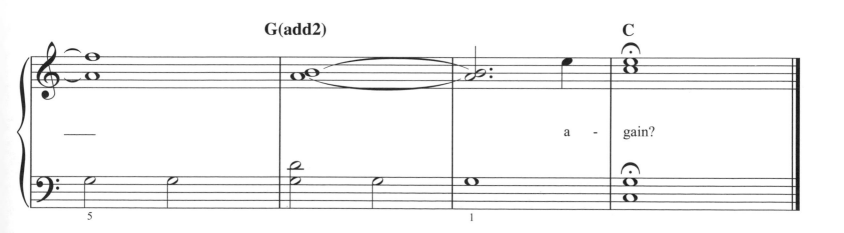

SWEETEST DEVOTION

Words and Music by ADELE ADKINS
and PAUL EPWORTH

Moderately slow

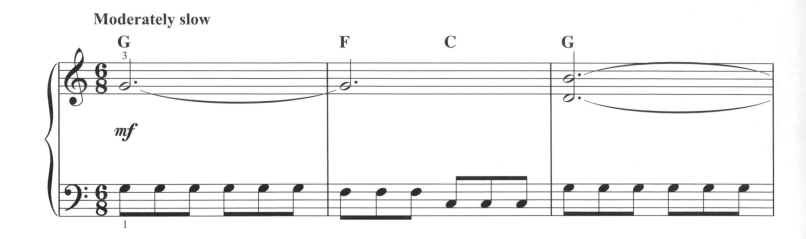

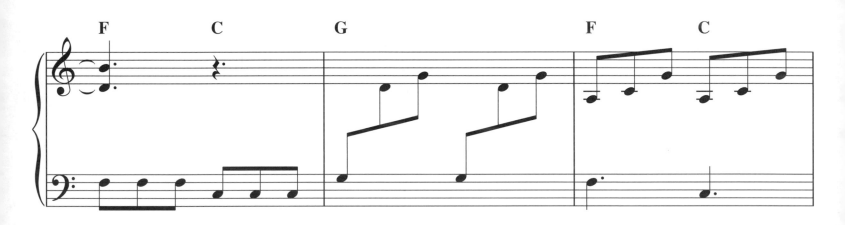

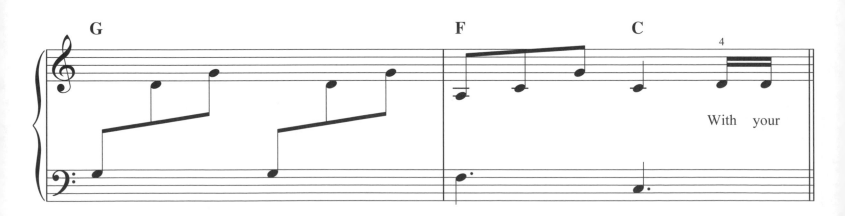

With your

lov - ing there ain't noth - ing that I can't a - dore. The way I'm
ev - er be what - ev - er you want me to be. I'd go

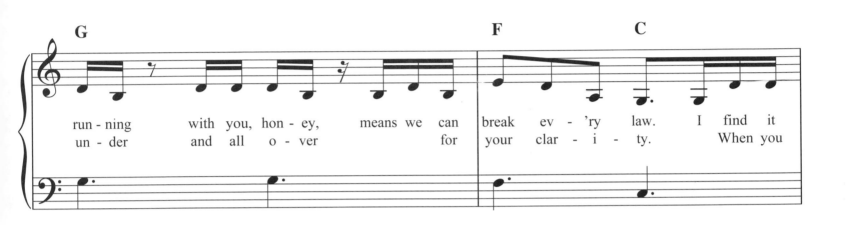

run - ning with you, hon - ey, means we can break ev - 'ry law. I find it
un - der and all o - ver for your clar - i - ty. When you

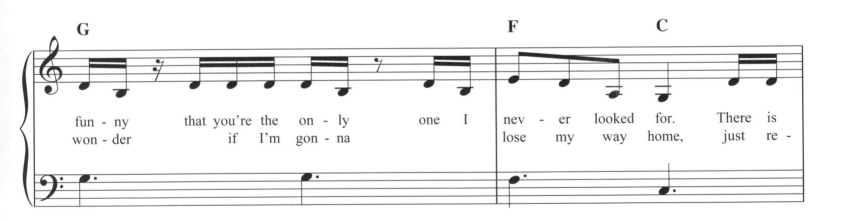

fun - ny that you're the on - ly one I nev - er looked for. There is
won - der if I'm gon - na lose my way home, just re -

some - thing in your lov - ing that tears down my walls. I weren't read - y then, I'm read - y now, I'm
mem - ber that come what - ev - er I'll be yours all a - long.

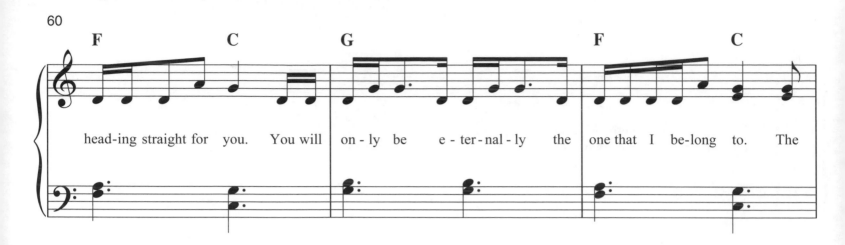

head-ing straight for you. You will on-ly be e-ter-nal-ly the one that I be-long to. The

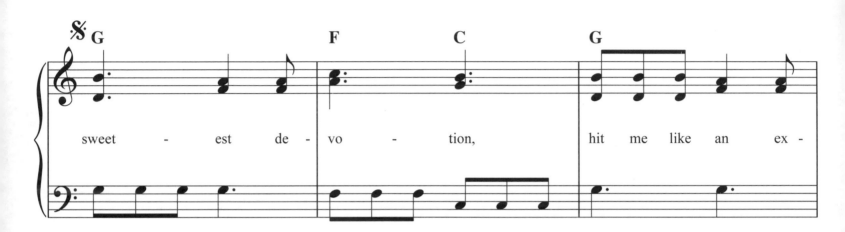

sweet - est de - vo - tion, hit me like an ex-

plo - sion. All of my life I've been fro - zen, the

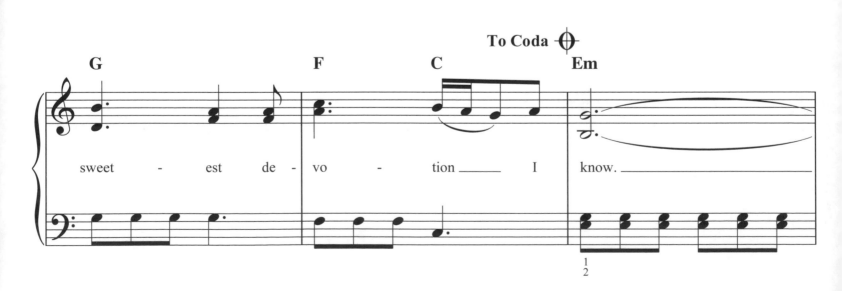

sweet - est de - vo - tion ____ I know. ____

look - ing for you, ba - by, in ev - 'ry face that I've ev - er known

and there is some - thing 'bout the way you love me that fi - nal - ly feels like

home. _____

G **Em**

You're my light, you're my

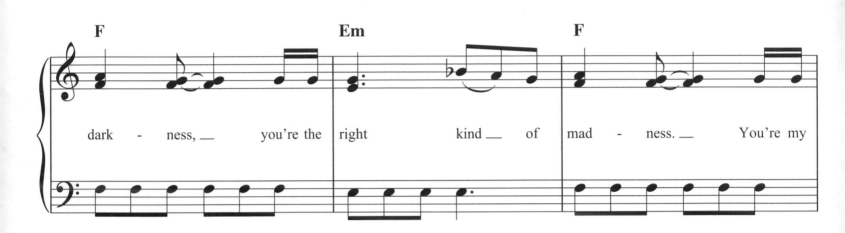

F **Em** **F**

dark - ness, __ you're the right kind __ of mad - ness. __ You're my

Em **F** **Em**

hope, you're my des - pair, __ you're my scope ev - 'ry - thing

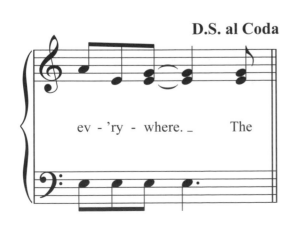

D.S. al Coda

ev - 'ry - where. _ The

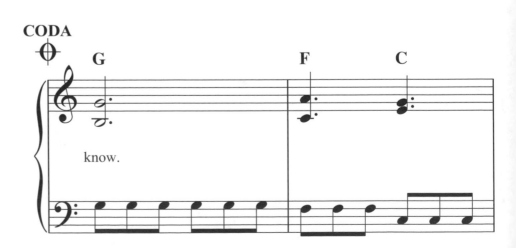

CODA

G **F** **C**

know.

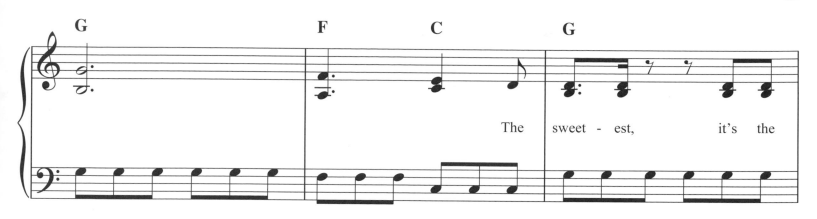

The sweet - est, it's the

sweet - est. The sweet - est, it's the sweet - est. The

sweet - est, it's the sweet - est. The sweet - est, it's the

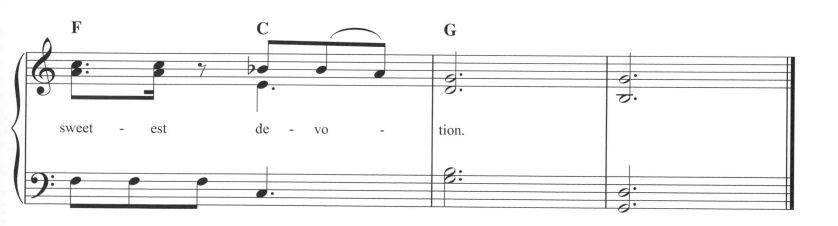

sweet - est de - vo - tion.